SOUP

SOUP

Hearty, simple soups for all seasons

CONTENTS

TECHNIQUES 6

RECIPES 8
Vegetable stock 8
Chicken stock 10
Fish stock 12
Brown meat stock 14
Gazpacho 16
Watercress soup 18
Curried parsnip soup 20
Borscht 22
Vichyssoise 24
Tomato soup 26
Mushroom soup 28
Carrot and orange soup 30
Porcini mushroom soup 32
White bean soup 34
Lobster bisque 36
Thick vegetable soup 38
Fish soup with saffron and fennel 40
Stracciatella with pasta 42
Tuscan bean soup 44
Hungarian goulash soup 46
French onion soup 48
Minestrone 50
New England clam chowder 52

Cock-a-leekie soup 54
Bouillabaisse 56
Winter vegetable soup 58
Sopa de tortilla 60
Chicken noodle soup 62
Lentil soup 64
Sweetcorn chowder 66
Pea and mint soup 68
Mussels in fennel broth 70
Chestnut and bacon soup 72
Bean and rosemary soup 74
Cauliflower soup 76
Black bean and coconut soup 78
Scotch broth 80
Asian turkey and noodle soup 82
Chilli beef and bean soup 84
Tomato and chorizo soup 86
Potato and leek soup 88
Spiced butternut squash soup 90
Split pea and bacon soup 92

INDEX 94
ACKNOWLEDGEMENTS 96

Guide to symbols

The recipes in this book are accompanied by symbols that alert you to important information.

 Tells you how many people the recipe serves, or how much is produced.

 Indicates how much time you will need to prepare and cook a dish. Next to this symbol you will also find out if additional time is required for such things as marinating, standing, proving, or cooling. You need to read the recipe to find out exactly how much extra time is needed.

 Alerts you to what has to be done before you can begin to cook the recipe, or to parts of the recipe that take a long time to complete.

 Denotes that special equipment is required. Where possible, alternatives are given.

 Accompanies freezing information.

Techniques

Make stock

A good stock is vital for a well-flavoured soup. Simply simmering a well-balanced combination of vegetables together produces a light, fragrant vegetable stock (see p8), or you can use bones to produce a gelatinous stock that is rich in flavour.

Chicken stock

1 Place either raw chicken bones, the whole carcass, or the bones and scraps from a cooked chicken in a large saucepan or stockpot with some aromatic vegetables and fresh herbs, and cover with water.

2 Bring to the boil, then reduce the heat and simmer for 2–3 hours, skimming off any foam that rises to the surface with a slotted spoon. Strain into a bowl through a fine sieve and leave to cool.

3 Once the stock has cooled, place it in the refrigerator. Any fat will congeal on the surface, and can then be removed with a slotted spoon. (See also Chicken stock recipe, p10.)

Fish stock

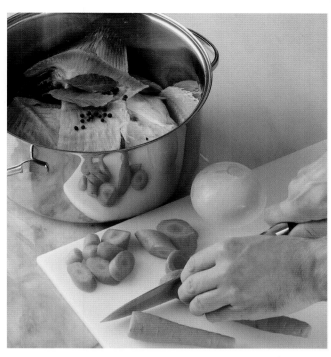

1 Put some fish trimmings and heads (blood rinsed off, bones cracked, trimmings cut into even-sized pieces) in a large pan. Avoid using oily fish such as mackerel, which produce an unpleasant flavour.

2 Roughly chop some aromatic vegetables (onions, celery, and carrots all work well) and add them to the pot, along with some fresh herbs. Cover with water and bring to the boil over a high heat.

3 Once the stock reaches the boil, lower the heat, and simmer for 20 minutes (any longer and the stock will start to become bitter). Skim off the scum that rises to the surface with a slotted spoon.

4 Ladle the stock through a fine sieve into a bowl, pressing the solid ingredients against the sieve to extract as much liquid as possible. Allow to cool, then refrigerate. (See also Fish stock recipe, p12.)

Vegetable stock

If you make more of this than you need, freeze any leftovers to use later.

INGREDIENTS

3 large carrots, scrubbed and coarsely
  chopped
3 large onions, coarsely chopped
3 large celery sticks, with leaves,
  coarsely chopped
2 leeks, chopped and rinsed
10 black peppercorns, lightly crushed
1 bunch of flat-leaf parsley, rinsed
2 bay leaves
½ tsp salt

METHOD

1 Put the carrots, onions, celery, and leeks in a large pan with 1.7 litres (3 pints) water. Bring to the boil. Use a slotted spoon to remove any foam that rises to the surface. Reduce the heat to low, then add the remaining ingredients, partially cover the pan, and simmer for 45 minutes, or until the stock is well flavoured.
2 Strain the stock into a large bowl, discarding the flavourings. The stock is now ready to use.

makes 1.2 litres (2 pints)

prep 10 mins • cook 1 hr

freeze for up to 6 months

Chicken stock

For a clear stock, make sure you remove any fat from the chicken before boiling, or it will turn cloudy. For a dark, golden stock, leave the onion unpeeled.

INGREDIENTS

1 chicken carcass, skin and fat removed
2 celery sticks, roughly chopped
1 onion, quartered
few sprigs of flat-leaf parsley
few sprigs of thyme
1 bay leaf
½ tsp salt
5 black peppercorns, lightly crushed

METHOD

1 Put the chicken pieces, celery, onion, herbs, and salt in a large pan with 2 litres (3½ pints) cold water and bring to boiling point over a high heat. Using a slotted spoon, skim off any foam as it rises to the surface. Reduce the heat to low, then add the peppercorns, partially cover the pan, and leave to simmer for about 1 hour.
2 Strain the stock into a large bowl, discarding the flavourings. It is now ready to use.

**makes 1 litre
(1¾ pints)**

**prep 10 mins
• cook 1 hr**

**freeze for
up to 6 months**

Fish stock

A tasty, delicate stock that is quick and easy to make.

INGREDIENTS
3 fish heads, plus bones and/or
  trimmings, any blood rinsed off and
  the bones cracked
2 onions, coarsely chopped
1 celery stick, coarsely chopped
few sprigs of thyme
few sprigs of flat-leaf parsley
1 bay leaf
¼ tsp salt

METHOD
1 Put 1.7 litres (3 pints) water, the fish trimmings, and onions into a large pan over a high heat and slowly bring to just below the boil. Use a slotted spoon to remove any foam as it rises to the surface.
2 Add the remaining ingredients, then partially cover the pan and leave to simmer for 20 minutes.
3 Strain the stock into a large bowl, discarding the flavourings. The stock is now ready to use.

makes 1.2 litres (2 pints)

prep 10 mins • cook 20 mins

freeze for up to 6 months

Brown meat stock

Use either beef or lamb bones for this rich stock,
but not a mixture of the two.

INGREDIENTS

1.35kg (3lb) beef or lamb bones, raw or
    cooked
2–3 onions, unpeeled and cut in half
2–3 carrots, cut in half
vegetable trimmings, such as
    mushrooms peelings, celery tops, or
    tomato skins

bacon rinds
bouquet garni, made with 1 celery stick,
    1 bay leaf, and a few sprigs of thyme
    and flat-leaf parsley
1 tbsp black peppercorns

METHOD

1 If the bones are raw, put them in a roasting tin with the onions and carrots, roast at
  200°C (400°F/Gas 6) oven for 30 minutes, or until browned, turning often. If you are
  using bones from cooked meat, omit this step.
2 Transfer the bones, onions, and carrots to a large saucepan, adding any vegetable
  trimmings, the bacon rinds, and the bouquet garni.
3 Pour in enough cold water to cover, and bring to the boil. Use a slotted spoon to
  remove any foam that rises to the surface. Lower the heat, add the peppercorns, and
  simmer for 3–4 hours.
4 Allow the stock to cool, then strain into a bowl or jug, discarding the flavourings. Chill
  overnight in the refrigerator so any fat solidifies on top and can be lifted off.

makes 2.5 litres
(4 pints)

prep 10 mins,
plus chilling
• cook 3½–4½ hrs

chill overnight to
separate the fat
from the liquid

freeze for
up to 6 months

Gazpacho

This chilled Spanish soup is always popular when the weather is hot.

INGREDIENTS

1 kg (2¼lb) tomatoes, plus extra to serve

1 small cucumber, peeled and finely chopped, plus extra to serve

1 small red pepper, deseeded and chopped, plus extra to serve

2 garlic cloves, crushed

4 tbsp sherry vinegar

salt and freshly ground black pepper

120ml (4fl oz) extra virgin olive oil, plus extra to serve

1 hard-boiled egg, white and yolk separated and chopped, to serve

METHOD

1 Bring a kettle of water to the boil. Place the tomatoes in a heatproof bowl, pour over enough boiling water to cover, and leave for 20 seconds, or until the skins split. Drain and cool under cold running water. Gently peel off the skins, cut the tomatoes in half, deseed, and chop the flesh.

2 Put the tomato flesh, cucumber, red pepper, garlic, and sherry vinegar in a food processor or blender. Season to taste with salt and pepper, and process until smooth. Pour in the olive oil and process again. Dilute with a little water if too thick. Transfer the soup to a serving bowl, cover with cling film, and chill for at least 1 hour.

3 When ready to serve, finely chop the extra cucumber and red pepper. Place the cucumber, pepper, and egg yolk and egg white in individual bowls and arrange on the table, along with a bottle of olive oil. Ladle the soup into bowls and serve, letting each diner add their own garnish.

serves 4

prep 15 mins, plus chilling

chill for at least 1 hr

food processor or blender

freeze, without the garnishes, for up to 1 month

Watercress soup

Serve this velvety smooth soup hot,
topped with Parmesan cheese.

INGREDIENTS

25g (scant 1 oz) butter
1 onion, peeled and finely chopped
175g (6 oz) watercress
3 ripe pears, cored and roughly chopped
1 litre (1¾ pints) vegetable stock
salt and freshly ground black pepper
200ml (7fl oz) double cream
juice of ½ lemon
Parmesan cheese, grated, to serve
olive oil, to drizzle

METHOD

1 Melt the butter in a saucepan and cook the onion for 10 minutes, or until soft, stirring occasionally to prevent burning.
2 Meanwhile, trim the watercress and pick off the leaves. Add the watercress stalks to the onion with the pears and stock, and season with salt and pepper.
3 Bring to the boil, cover and simmer gently for 15 minutes. Remove from the heat and pour into a blender along with the watercress leaves. Process until the soup has a very smooth texture.
4 Stir in the cream and lemon juice, adjust the seasoning, and serve sprinkled with Parmesan and drizzled with a little oil.

serves 4

prep 10 mins • cook 15 mins

blender

freeze the soup, before the cream is added, for up to 3 months

Curried parsnip soup

Gentle spices perk up this earthy-flavoured soup.

INGREDIENTS

1 onion
300g (10 oz) parsnips
1 carrot
1 potato
45g (1½ oz) butter
2 tbsp plain flour
2 tbsp mild curry powder
1.2 litres (2 pints) vegetable stock or
  water
crème fraîche, to serve
flat-leaf parsley, chopped, to serve

METHOD

1 Peel and roughly chop all the vegetables, keeping the onion separate.
2 Melt the butter in a large saucepan over a medium heat; add the onion, and cook, stirring frequently, until it is soft but not browned. Add the other vegetables, followed by the flour and curry powder, and cook, stirring, for a further 2 minutes.
3 Gradually add the stock or water, stirring until well blended. Increase the heat and bring to the boil, then reduce the heat to a low simmer. Cover and leave to cook for 40 minutes.
4 Turn the heat off, uncover, and allow the soup to cool slightly. Pour the soup into a blender or food processor and purée until completely smooth.
5 Reheat before serving, then pour into individual bowls. Add a swirl of crème fraîche and a scattering of chopped parsley.

serves 4

prep 10 mins • cook 50 mins

blender or food processor

Borscht

This classic Russian soup is thickly textured and satisfying.

INGREDIENTS

2 large beetroot
1 onion
1 carrot
1 celery stick
45g (1½ oz) butter or goose fat
400g can chopped tomatoes
1 garlic clove, crushed (optional)

1.7 litres (3 pints) vegetable stock
2 bay leaves
4 cloves
2 tbsp lemon juice
salt and freshly ground black pepper
200ml (7fl oz) soured cream (optional)

METHOD

1 Roughly grate the beetroot, onion, carrot, and celery stick.
2 Melt the butter in a large saucepan over a medium heat. Add the vegetables and cook, stirring, for 5 minutes, or until just softened.
3 Add the tomatoes and crushed garlic, if using, and cook for 2–3 minutes, stirring frequently, then stir in the stock.
4 Tie the bay leaves and cloves in a small piece of muslin and add to the pan. Bring the soup to the boil, then reduce the heat, cover, and simmer for 1 hour 20 minutes.
5 Discard the muslin bag. Stir in the lemon juice and season to taste with salt and pepper.
6 Ladle the soup into warm bowls and add a swirl of soured cream to each, if using.

serves 4

**prep 15 mins
• cook 1 hr
30 mins**

muslin

Vichyssoise

Despite its French name, this silky, smooth iced soup originates from America and may also be served hot.

INGREDIENTS

30g (1 oz) butter

3 large leeks, green ends discarded, finely sliced

2 potatoes, about 175g (6 oz) in total, peeled and chopped

1 celery stick, roughly chopped

1.2 litres (2 pints) vegetable stock

salt and freshly ground black pepper

150ml (5fl oz) double cream, plus extra to serve

2 tbsp finely chopped chives, to serve

METHOD

1 Heat the butter in a heavy saucepan over a medium heat and add the leeks. Press a piece of damp greaseproof paper on top, cover, and cook, shaking gently from time to time, for 15 minutes, or until the leeks are softened and golden.

2 Add the potatoes, celery, and stock, and season with salt and pepper. Bring to the boil, stirring, then cover and simmer for 30 minutes, or until the vegetables are tender.

3 Remove the pan from the heat and leave to cool slightly, then process in a blender until very smooth, in batches if necessary. Season to taste with salt and pepper and allow the soup to cool completely before stirring in the cream. Chill for at least 3 hours before serving.

4 To serve, pour into serving bowls, lightly stir in a little extra cream, and sprinkle with chives and black pepper.

serves 4

prep 15 mins, plus chilling
• cook 45 mins

chill for at least 3 hrs

blender

freeze, before the cream is added, for up to 3 months

Tomato soup

Easy to make, this delicious soup can be enjoyed all year round.

INGREDIENTS
1 tbsp olive oil
1 onion, chopped
1 garlic clove, sliced
2 celery sticks, sliced
1 carrot, sliced
1 potato, chopped
2 x 400g cans tomatoes
750ml (1¼ pints) vegetable stock or
   chicken stock
1 bay leaf
1 tsp sugar
salt and freshly ground black pepper

METHOD
1 Heat the oil in a large saucepan over a medium-low heat, add the onion, garlic, and celery, and fry, stirring frequently, until softened but not coloured.
2 Add the carrot and potato and stir for 1 minute, then add the tomatoes with their juice, stock, bay leaf, and sugar. Season to taste with salt and pepper, bring to the boil, then reduce the heat, cover, and simmer for 45 minutes, or until the vegetables are very soft.
3 Remove from the heat, discard the bay leaf, and allow to cool slightly, then process in a blender or food processor until smooth, working in batches if necessary. Taste and adjust the seasoning, then reheat and serve. Garnish with celery leaves and swirls of double cream, if you like.

serves 4

prep 20 mins
• cook 55 mins

blender or
food processor

Mushroom soup

Using a selection of both wild and cultivated mushrooms will produce a soup that is bursting with flavour.

INGREDIENTS

30g (1 oz) butter
1 onion, finely chopped
2 celery sticks, finely chopped
1 garlic clove, crushed
450g (1lb) mixed mushrooms, roughly chopped
200g (7 oz) potatoes, peeled and cubed
1 litre (1¾ pints) vegetable stock
2 tbsp finely chopped flat-leaf parsley
salt and freshly ground black pepper

METHOD

1 Melt the butter in a large saucepan, add the onion, celery, and garlic, and fry for 3–4 minutes, or until softened.
2 Stir in the mushrooms and continue to fry for a further 5–6 minutes. Add the potatoes and stock and bring up to the boil. Reduce the heat and leave to simmer gently for 30 minutes.
3 Use a hand blender to process the soup until smooth. Sprinkle in the parsley and season to taste with salt and pepper. Serve immediately.

serves 4

prep 10 mins • cook 45 mins

hand blender

freeze for up to 3 months

Carrot and orange soup

A light, refreshing soup with a hint of spice –
this is perfect for summer.

INGREDIENTS

2 tsp light olive oil or sunflower oil

1 leek, sliced

500g (1lb 2 oz) carrots, sliced

1 potato, about 115g (4 oz), chopped

½ tsp ground coriander

pinch of ground cumin

300ml (10fl oz) orange juice

500ml (16fl oz) vegetable stock or
chicken stock

1 bay leaf

salt and freshly ground black pepper

2 tbsp chopped coriander, to garnish

METHOD

1 Place the oil, leek, and carrots in a large saucepan and cook over a low heat for
5 minutes, stirring frequently, or until the leek has softened. Add the potato, coriander,
and cumin, then pour in the orange juice and stock. Add the bay leaf and stir.

2 Increase the heat, bring the soup to the boil, then lower the heat, cover, and simmer for
40 minutes, or until the vegetables are very tender.

3 Allow the soup to cool slightly, discard the bay leaf, then transfer to a blender or food
processor and process until smooth, working in batches if necessary.

4 Return to the saucepan and add a little extra stock or water if the soup is too thick.
Bring back to a simmer, then transfer to heated serving bowls and sprinkle with
chopped coriander. Garnish with a drizzling of double cream, if you like.

serves 4

prep 10 mins
• cook 40 mins

blender or
food processor

Porcini mushroom soup

This hearty Italian country soup is full of deep, earthy goodness.

INGREDIENTS

30g (1 oz) dried porcini mushrooms
3 tbsp extra virgin olive oil, plus extra to finish
2 onions, finely chopped
2 tsp chopped rosemary leaves
1 tsp thyme leaves
2 garlic cloves, finely sliced
115g (4 oz) chestnut mushrooms, sliced

2 celery sticks with leaves, finely chopped
400g (14 oz) can chopped tomatoes
750ml (1¼ pints) vegetable stock
salt and freshly ground black pepper
½ stale ciabatta or small crusty white loaf, torn into chunks

METHOD

1 Put the dried porcini in a heatproof bowl, pour over 300ml (10fl oz) boiling water, and leave to stand for 30 minutes. Drain, reserving the soaking liquid, then chop any large pieces of mushroom.

2 Heat the oil in a saucepan, add the onions, cover, and leave to cook for 10 minutes, or until soft. Add the rosemary, thyme, garlic, chestnut mushrooms, and celery, and continue cooking, uncovered, until the celery has softened.

3 Add the tomatoes, porcini, and stock. Strain the reserved soaking liquid through muslin or a fine sieve into the pan. Bring to the boil, then lower the heat and simmer gently for 45 minutes.

4 Season to taste with salt and pepper, and add the bread. Remove the pan from the heat. Cover and leave to stand for 10 minutes before serving. Spoon into deep bowls and drizzle each serving with a little olive oil.

serves 4

prep 20 mins, plus standing • cook 1 hr

freeze, without the bread, for up to 3 months

White bean soup

This thick soup from northern Italy is guaranteed to keep out the winter chills.

INGREDIENTS

3 tbsp olive oil

2 onions, finely chopped

2 garlic cloves, crushed

225g (8 oz) dried cannellini beans, soaked overnight

1 celery stick, chopped

1 bay leaf

3 or 4 parsley stalks, without leaves

1 tbsp lemon juice

1.2 litres (2 pints) vegetable stock

salt and freshly ground black pepper

3 shallots, thinly sliced

60g (2 oz) pancetta, chopped (optional)

85g (3 oz) fontina cheese or Taleggio cheese, chopped into small pieces

METHOD

1 Heat 2 tablespoons of the olive oil in a saucepan, add the onions, and fry over a low heat for 10 minutes, or until softened, stirring occasionally. Add the garlic and cook, stirring, for 1 minute.

2 Drain the soaked beans and add to the pan with the celery, bay leaf, parsley stalks, lemon juice, and stock. Bring to the boil, cover, and simmer for 1½ hours, or until the beans are soft, stirring occasionally.

3 Remove the bay leaf and liquidize the soup in batches in a blender, or through a hand mill. Rinse out the pan. Return the soup to the pan and season to taste with salt and pepper.

4 Heat the remaining olive oil in a small frying pan, and fry the shallots and pancetta (if using), until golden and crisp, stirring frequently to stop them sticking to the pan.

5 Reheat the soup, adding a little stock or water if it is too thick. Stir the cheese into the soup. Ladle into individual bowls, and sprinkle each serving with the shallots and pancetta.

 serves 4

 prep 30 mins, plus soaking • cook 2 hrs

 soak the beans overnight to rehydrate them

 blender or hand mill

Lobster bisque

The name "bisque" refers to a shellfish soup with cream and is thought to have come from the Spanish Biscay region.

INGREDIENTS

1 lobster, cooked, about 1kg (2¼lb) in weight
50g (1¾ oz) butter
1 tbsp olive oil
1 onion, finely chopped
1 carrot, finely chopped
2 celery sticks, finely chopped
1 leek, finely chopped
½ fennel bulb, finely chopped
1 bay leaf
1 sprig of tarragon

2 garlic cloves, crushed
75g (2½ oz) tomato purée
4 tomatoes, roughly chopped
120ml (4fl oz) Cognac or brandy
100ml (3½fl oz) dry white wine or vermouth
1.7 litres (3 pints) fish stock
120ml (4fl oz) cream
salt and freshly ground black pepper
pinch of cayenne pepper

METHOD

1 Split the lobster in half, remove the meat from the body, and chop the meat into small pieces. Twist off the claws and legs, break the claws at the joints, and crack the shells with the back of a knife. Chop the shell into rough pieces.

2 Melt the butter with the oil in a large saucepan over a medium heat, add the vegetables, herbs, and garlic, and cook for 10 minutes, or until softened, stirring occasionally.

3 Add the chopped lobster shells. Stir in the tomato purée, chopped tomatoes, Cognac, white wine, and fish stock. Bring to the boil and simmer for 1 hour.

4 Leave to cool slightly, then ladle into a food processor with the lobster meat. Process the soup in short bursts until the shell breaks into very small pieces.

5 Strain the soup through a coarse sieve, pushing as much liquid through as you can. Then pass the soup again through a fine mesh sieve before returning to the heat.

6 Bring to the boil, add the cream, then season to taste with salt and pepper and add cayenne pepper and lemon juice to taste. Serve in warm bowls, garnished with chives.

serves 4

prep 45 mins • cook 1 hr 10 mins

food processor

freeze for up to 3 months

Thick vegetable soup

This filling soup is a good winter warmer.

INGREDIENTS

2 tbsp olive oil

2 onions, finely chopped

salt and freshly ground black pepper

4 garlic cloves, grated or finely chopped

1 tbsp rosemary leaves, finely chopped

4 celery sticks, finely chopped

4 carrots, finely chopped

4 courgettes, finely chopped

2 x 400g cans whole tomatoes, chopped
  in the can

1.2 litres (2 pints) hot vegetable stock

handful of flat-leaf parsley, finely
  chopped

METHOD

1 Heat the oil in a large pan, add the onions, and cook over a low heat for 6–8 minutes, or until soft and translucent. Season with salt and black pepper, then add the garlic, rosemary, celery, and carrots and cook over a low heat, stirring occasionally, for 10 minutes.

2 Add the courgettes and cook for 5 minutes, then stir in the tomatoes, and squash with the back of a fork. Add the stock, bring to the boil, then reduce to a simmer and cook for 20 minutes. Season well with salt and pepper, then stir through the parsley. Serve with fresh crusty bread.

serves 8

**prep 15 mins
• cook 45 mins**

**freeze for up
to 3 months**

Fish soup with saffron & fennel

This rustic soup is simple to prepare and sure to please.

INGREDIENTS

30g (1 oz) butter
3 tbsp olive oil
1 large fennel bulb, finely chopped
2 garlic cloves, crushed
1 small leek, sliced
4 ripe plum tomatoes, chopped
3 tbsp brandy
¼ tsp saffron threads, soaked in
  a little hot water
zest of ½ orange
1 bay leaf

1.7 litres (3 pints) fish stock
300g (10 oz) potatoes, diced and
  parboiled for 5 minutes
4 tbsp dry white wine
500g (1lb 2oz) fresh black mussels,
  scrubbed and debearded
salt and freshly ground black pepper
500g (1lb 2oz) monkfish or firm white
  fish, cut into bite-sized pieces
6 raw whole tiger prawns
flat-leaf parsley, chopped, to serve

METHOD

1 Heat the butter with 2 tablespoons of the oil in a large, deep pan. Stir in the fennel, garlic, and leek, and fry over a moderate heat, stirring occasionally, for 5 minutes, or until softened and lightly browned.

2 Stir in the tomatoes, add the brandy, and boil rapidly for 2 minutes, or until the juices are reduced slightly. Stir in the saffron in its water, orange zest, bay leaf, fish stock, and potatoes. Bring to the boil, then reduce the heat and skim off any scum from the surface. Cover and simmer for 20 minutes, or until the potatoes are tender. Remove the bay leaf.

3 Meanwhile, heat the remaining oil with the wine in a large deep pan until boiling. Add the mussels, cover, and continue cooking on a high heat for 2–3 minutes, shaking the pan often. Discard any mussels that do not open. Strain, reserving the liquid, and set the mussels aside.

4 Add the liquid to the soup and season to taste with salt and pepper. Bring to the boil, add the monkfish pieces and prawns, then reduce the heat, cover, and simmer gently for 5 minutes, or until the fish is just cooked and the prawns are pink. Add the mussels to the pan and bring almost to the boil.

5 Serve the soup sprinkled with chopped parsley.

serves 4–6

prep 10 mins
• cook 1 hr

before cooking, tap the
mussels and discard
any that do not close

Stracciatella with pasta

A flavoursome soup that makes a perfect light lunch.

INGREDIENTS

1.5 litres (2¾ pints) chicken stock
100g (3½ oz) soup pasta
4 eggs
salt and freshly ground black pepper
½ tsp freshly grated nutmeg
2 tbsp grated Parmesan cheese
1 tbsp chopped flat-leaf parsley
1 tbsp olive oil

METHOD

1 Place the stock in a large pan and bring to the boil. Add the pasta and cook according to packet directions, or until cooked but still firm to the bite.

2 Break the eggs into a small bowl, add the nutmeg, season with salt and pepper, and whisk lightly with a fork to break up the egg. Add the Parmesan and parsley.

3 Add the olive oil to the simmering stock, reduce the heat to low, then stir the stock lightly to create a gentle "whirlpool". Gradually pour in the eggs and cook for 1 minute, without boiling, so they set into fine strands. Leave to stand for 1 minute before serving.

serves 4–6

prep 10 mins
• cook 20 mins

Tuscan bean soup

This classic dish, *Ribollita*, is named after the traditional method of re-boiling soup from the day before. The flavours will improve if made a day in advance.

INGREDIENTS

4 tbsp extra virgin olive oil, plus extra
  for drizzling
1 onion, chopped
2 carrots, sliced
1 leek, sliced
2 garlic cloves, chopped
400g can chopped tomatoes
1 tbsp tomato purée
900ml (1½ pints) chicken stock

salt and freshly ground black pepper
400g can borlotti beans, flageolet
  beans, or cannellini beans, drained
  and rinsed
250g (9 oz) baby spinach leaves or
  spring greens, shredded
8 slices ciabatta bread
grated Parmesan cheese, for sprinkling

METHOD

1 Heat the oil in a large saucepan and fry the onion, carrots, and leek over a low heat for 10 minutes, or until softened but not coloured. Add the garlic and fry for 1 minute. Add the tomatoes, tomato purée, and stock. Season to taste with salt and pepper.
2 Mash half the beans with a fork and add to the pan. Bring to the boil, then lower the heat and simmer for 30 minutes.
3 Add the remaining beans and spinach to the pan. Simmer for a further 30 minutes.
4 Toast the bread until golden and drizzle with olive oil. Spoon the soup into the bowls, top with a sprinkling of Parmesan, drizzle with a little more olive oil, and serve with the toast.

serves 4

prep 15 mins
• cook 1 hr
20 mins

Hungarian goulash soup

A traditional, warming soup flavoured with beef, onions, tomato, and paprika.

INGREDIENTS

120ml (4fl oz) olive oil
675g (1½ lb) onions, peeled and sliced
2 garlic cloves, crushed
675g (1½ lb) chuck steak, cut into 5cm (2 in) cubes
salt and freshly ground black pepper
2 tbsp paprika

1 tsp caraway seeds
1 tsp cayenne pepper, plus extra, for sprinkling
4 tbsp tomato purée
1 litre (1¾ pints) beef stock
soured cream, to serve

METHOD

1 Heat a large flameproof casserole over medium heat with 3 tablespoons of the olive oil and cook the onions for 10 minutes, or until golden brown. Add the garlic for the final 2 minutes, stirring occasionally.

2 Meanwhile, in a separate pan, heat the remaining oil and brown the meat on all sides.

3 Season the meat with salt and add it to the onions, along with the spices and tomato purée. Cook for 5 minutes, stirring all the time, before adding the stock.

4 Simmer gently for 1 hour 45 minutes, or until the meat is very tender. Season to taste with salt and pepper, and serve with soured cream and a sprinkling of cayenne pepper.

serves 6–8

prep 15 mins • cook 2 hrs

large flameproof casserole

French onion soup

This Parisian classic is given extra punch with spoonfuls of brandy.

INGREDIENTS

30g (1 oz) butter

1 tbsp sunflower oil

675g (1½ lb) onions, thinly sliced

1 tsp sugar

salt and freshly ground black pepper

120ml (4fl oz) red wine

2 tbsp plain white flour

1.5 litres (2¾ pints) beef stock

4 tbsp brandy

1 garlic clove, cut in half

4 slices of baguette, about 2cm (¾in) thick, toasted

115g (4 oz) Gruyère cheese or Emmental cheese, grated

METHOD

1 Melt the butter with the oil in a large, heavy pan over a low heat. Stir together the onions and sugar and season to taste with salt and pepper. Press a piece of wet, greaseproof paper over the surface and cook, stirring occasionally, uncovered, for 40 minutes, or until the onions are rich and dark golden brown. Take care that they do not stick and burn on the bottom.

2 Remove the paper and stir in the wine. Increase the heat to medium and stir for 5 minutes, or until the onions are glazed. Sprinkle with the flour and stir for 2 minutes. Stir in the stock and bring to the boil. Reduce the heat to low, cover, and leave the soup to simmer for 30 minutes. Taste and adjust the seasoning, if necessary.

3 Meanwhile, preheat the grill on its highest setting. Divide the soup between 4 flameproof bowls and stir 1 tablespoon of brandy into each. Rub the garlic clove over the toast and place 1 slice in each bowl. Sprinkle with the cheese and grill for 2–3 minutes, or until the cheese is bubbling and golden. Serve at once.

serves 4

prep 10 mins
• cook 1 hr
20 mins

flameproof
soup bowls

❄ freeze the soup, without the bread or cheese, for up to 1 month

Minestrone

You can add whatever vegetables are in season to this substantial soup.

INGREDIENTS

100g (3½ oz) dried white cannellini beans, soaked for at least 6 hours, or overnight
2 tbsp olive oil
2 celery sticks, finely chopped
2 carrots, finely chopped
1 onion, finely chopped
400g can chopped tomatoes

750ml (1¼ pints) chicken stock or vegetable stock
salt and freshly ground black pepper
60g (2 oz) small short-cut pasta
4 tbsp chopped flat-leaf parsley
45g (1½ oz) Parmesan cheese, finely grated

METHOD

1 Drain the soaked beans, place in a large saucepan, cover with cold water, and bring to the boil over a high heat, skimming the surface as necessary. Boil for 10 minutes, then reduce the heat to low, partially cover the pan, and leave the beans to simmer for 1 hour, or until just tender. Drain well and set aside. Rinse the pan.

2 Heat the oil in the rinsed-out pan over a medium heat. Add the celery, carrots, and onion and fry, stirring occasionally, for 5 minutes, or until tender. Stir in the beans, the tomatoes with their juice, and the stock, and season to taste with salt and pepper. Bring to the boil, stirring, then cover and leave to simmer for 20 minutes.

3 Add the pasta and simmer for a further 10–15 minutes, or until cooked but still firm to the bite. Stir in the parsley and half the Parmesan, then adjust the seasoning. Serve hot, sprinkled with the remaining Parmesan.

serves 4–6

prep 20 mins, plus soaking
• cook 1 hr 45 mins

soak the beans for at least 6 hrs to rehydrate them

freeze, before the pasta is added, for up to 1 month

New England clam chowder

Americans often serve this traditional, creamy soup with small saltine crackers.

INGREDIENTS

36 live clams

1 tbsp oil

115g (4 oz) thick-cut rindless streaky bacon rashers, diced

1 onion, finely chopped

2 floury potatoes, such as King Edward, peeled and cut into 1cm (½in) cubes

2 tbsp plain white flour

600ml (1 pint) whole milk

salt and freshly ground black pepper

125ml (4½fl oz) single cream

2 tbsp finely chopped flat-leaf parsley

METHOD

1 Discard any open clams. Shuck the clams and reserve the juice, adding enough water to make 600ml (1 pint). Chop the clams.

2 Heat the oil in a large, heavy saucepan. Fry the bacon over a medium heat, stirring frequently, for 5 minutes, or until crisp. Remove the bacon from the pan with a slotted spoon, drain on kitchen paper and set aside.

3 Add the onion and potatoes to the pan and fry for 5 minutes, or until the onion has softened. Add the flour and cook, stirring for 2 minutes.

4 Stir in the clam juice and milk and season to taste with salt and pepper. Bring to the boil, cover the pan, reduce the heat, and leave to simmer for 20 minutes or until the potatoes are tender. Add the clams and simmer gently, uncovered, for 5 minutes.

5 Stir in the cream and heat through without boiling. Serve hot, sprinkled with the bacon and parsley.

 serves 4

 prep 15 mins • cook 35 mins

 before cooking, tap the clams and discard any that do not close

Cock-a-leekie soup

The traditional method involves the slow simmering of a whole chicken, but today it can be prepared with less time and effort.

INGREDIENTS

450g (1lb) chicken breasts and thighs, skinned
2 bay leaves
1 litre (1¾ pints) chicken stock or vegetable stock
2 leeks, thinly sliced
2 carrots, grated
60g (2 oz) long-grain rice
pinch of ground cloves
1 tsp sea salt
1 tbsp chopped flat-leaf parsley

METHOD

1 Place the chicken in a pan with the bay leaves and pour in the stock. Bring to the boil then reduce the heat, cover, and simmer for 30 minutes.
2 Skim the surface of the soup and discard any scum that has formed. Add the vegetables, rice, cloves, and salt, bring back to the boil, reduce the heat, cover, and simmer for a further 30 minutes.
3 Remove the bay leaves and discard. If you wish, you can lift out the chicken, remove the meat from the bones, then return the meat to the soup.
4 Stir in the parsley, then ladle the soup into a warm tureen or divide between individual serving bowls and serve while still hot.

serves 4

prep 10 mins • cook 1 hr

freeze for up to 3 months

Bouillabaisse

INGREDIENTS

4 tbsp olive oil

1 onion, thinly sliced

2 leeks, thinly sliced

1 small fennel bulb, thinly sliced

2–3 garlic cloves, finely chopped

4 tomatoes, skinned, deseeded, and chopped

1 tbsp tomato purée

250ml (9fl oz) dry white wine

1.5 litres (2¾ pints) fish stock or chicken stock

pinch of saffron threads

strip of orange zest

1 bouquet garni

salt and freshly ground black pepper

1.35kg (3lb) mixed white and oily fish and shellfish, such as gurnard, John Dory, monkfish, red mullet, prawns, and mussels, heads and bones removed

2 tbsp Pernod

8 thin slices day-old French bread, toasted, to serve

For the rouille

125g (4½ oz) mayonnaise

1 bird's-eye chilli, deseeded and roughly chopped

4 garlic cloves, roughly chopped

1 tbsp tomato purée

½ tsp salt

METHOD

1 Heat the oil in a large saucepan over a medium heat. Add the onion, leeks, fennel, and garlic and fry, stirring frequently, for 5–8 minutes, or until the vegetables are softened but not coloured. Add the tomatoes, tomato purée, and wine and stir until blended.

2 Add the stock, saffron, orange zest, and bouquet garni. Season to taste with salt and pepper, and bring to the boil. Reduce the heat, partially cover the pan, and simmer for 30 minutes, or until the soup is reduced slightly, stirring occasionally.

3 To make the rouille, place all ingredients into a blender or food processor and process until smooth. Transfer to a bowl, cover with cling film, and chill until required.

4 Just before the liquid finishes simmering, cut the fish into chunks. Remove the orange zest and bouquet garni from the soup and add the firm fish. Reduce the heat to low and let the soup simmer for 5 minutes, then add the delicate fish and simmer for a further 2–3 minutes, or until all the fish is cooked through and flakes easily. Stir in the Pernod, and season to taste with salt and pepper.

5 To serve, spread each piece of toast with rouille and put 2 slices in the bottom of each bowl. Ladle the soup on top and serve.

serves 4

prep 20 mins
• cook 45 mins

before cooking, tap the mussels and discard any that do not close

blender or food processor

Winter vegetable soup

Some people call this "Penny Soup", not just because it is inexpensive to make but because the vegetables resemble coins.

INGREDIENTS
1 leek
300g (10 oz) new potatoes
250g (9 oz) large carrots
175g (6 oz) small sweet potatoes
15g (½ oz) butter
1 tbsp olive oil
600ml (1 pint) vegetable stock
1 tbsp chopped flat-leaf parsley
  (optional)
salt and freshly ground black pepper

METHOD
1 Slice all the vegetables across into rounds about 2–3mm (⅛in) thick. The potatoes can be left peeled or unpeeled.
2 Melt the butter with the oil in a large saucepan or flameproof casserole and add the leeks. Cook over a medium heat for 3–4 minutes, or until soft, stirring frequently. Add the remaining vegetables and cook, stirring, for 1 minute.
3 Pour in the stock, bring to the boil, cover, and simmer for 18–20 minutes, or until the vegetables are tender but not soft.
4 Transfer about a third of the vegetables into a blender or food processor with a little of the liquid. Blend to a smooth purée and return to the pan. Stir in the parsley (if using), season to taste with salt and pepper, and serve, with the vegetables in a little mound in the centre.

serves 4

prep 15 mins
• cook 25 mins

blender or
food processor

Sopa de tortilla

Fresh lime juice, coriander, and dried poblano chillies give a Mexican flavour to this tomato soup.

INGREDIENTS

5 tbsp sunflower oil

½ onion, finely chopped

2 large garlic cloves, finely chopped

450g (1lb) tomatoes, skinned

1.5 litres (2¾ pints) chicken stock or vegetable stock

1 or 2 dried poblano chillies, deseeded

2 soft corn tortillas, cut into strips

3 tbsp chopped coriander

2 tbsp fresh lime juice

salt and freshly ground black pepper

85g (3 oz) Gruyère cheese, grated

2 limes, cut into wedges, to serve

METHOD

1 Heat 1 tablespoon of the oil in a large saucepan over a medium heat. Add the onion and fry, stirring, for 5 minutes, or until softened. Add the garlic and stir for 30 seconds. Transfer to a food processor or blender with the tomatoes and process until smooth.

2 Tip the purée into the pan and simmer for 8–10 minutes, stirring constantly. Stir in the stock and bring to the boil. Reduce the heat, partially cover the pan, and simmer for 15 minutes, or until the soup has thickened.

3 Place a non-stick frying pan over a medium heat. Add the chillies and press them flat against the pan with a spatula until they blister, then repeat for the other side. Remove from the pan, cut into small pieces, and set aside.

4 Heat the remaining oil in the frying pan until sizzling hot. Add the tortilla strips in batches and fry just until crisp. Remove with a slotted spoon and drain on kitchen paper.

5 When ready to serve, add the chillies to the soup, bring to the boil and simmer for 3 minutes, or until the chillies are soft. Stir in the coriander and lime juice and salt and pepper to taste. Divide the toasted tortilla strips between 4 soup bowls. Ladle in the soup, top with a sprinkling of cheese, and serve with lime wedges.

serves 4

prep 15 mins • cook 50 mins

food processor or blender

Chicken noodle soup

This spicy Mexican soup, *Sopa Seca de Fideos*, is made with thin fideo noodles, which are similar to angel hair pasta.

INGREDIENTS

2 large ripe tomatoes, skinned and deseeded

2 garlic cloves

1 small onion, roughly chopped

2 dried chipotle chillies, soaked

900ml (1½ pints) chicken stock

3 tbsp vegetable oil

2 skinless boneless chicken breasts, diced

225g (8 oz) Mexican fideo or dried angel hair pasta

4 tbsp soured cream, to serve

1 avocado, stone removed and chopped, to serve

METHOD

1 Put the tomatoes, garlic, onion, chillies, and 2 tablespoons of stock into a food processor or blender, and process to a purée. Set aside.

2 Heat 2 tablespoons of oil in a large pan and stir-fry the chicken for 2–3 minutes, or until just cooked. Remove from the pan, drain on kitchen paper, and set aside.

3 Add the remaining oil to the pan, add the noodles, and cook over a low heat until the noodles are golden, stirring constantly.

4 Pour in the tomato mixture, stir until the noodles are coated, then add the stock, and return the chicken to the pan. Cook the noodles for 2–3 minutes, or until just tender.

5 To serve, ladle into soup bowls, and top each with soured cream and chopped avocado.

serves 4

prep 20 mins
• cook 15 mins

soak the dried chillies in water for 30 mins before using

food processor or blender

Lentil soup

This hearty vegetarian soup has just a touch of spice.

INGREDIENTS

1 tbsp olive oil
2 onions, finely chopped
2 celery sticks, finely chopped
2 carrots, finely chopped
2 garlic cloves, crushed
1–2 tsp curry powder
150g (5½ oz) red lentils
1.4 litres (2½ pints) vegetable stock
120ml (4fl oz) tomato juice or vegetable
   juice
salt and freshly ground black pepper

METHOD

1 Heat the oil in a large pan over a medium heat, then add the onions, celery, and
   carrots. Cook, stirring, for 5 minutes, or until the onions are soft and translucent.
2 Add the garlic and curry powder and cook, stirring, for a further 1 minute, then add
   the lentils, stock, and tomato juice.
3 Bring to the boil, then lower the heat, cover, and simmer for 25 minutes, or until the
   vegetables are tender. Season to taste with salt and pepper, and serve hot with
   crusty bread.

serves 4

**prep 20 mins
• cook 35 mins**

Sweetcorn chowder

Full of potatoes and sweetcorn, this is a simple but tasty, chunky soup.

INGREDIENTS

2 tbsp olive oil
2 onions, finely chopped
salt and freshly ground black pepper
6–8 medium potatoes, cut into
  bite-sized pieces
2 x 340g cans sweetcorn, drained
1.4 litres (2½ pints) hot vegetable stock
handful of flat-leaf parsley, finely
  chopped
4 tbsp double cream (optional), to serve

METHOD

1 Heat the oil in a large pan, add the onions, and cook over a low heat for 6–8 minutes, or until soft and translucent. Season well with salt and black pepper, then stir in the potatoes and cook over a low heat for 5 minutes.
2 Mash the sweetcorn a little with the back of a fork, then add to the pan. Pour in the stock, bring to the boil, then reduce to a simmer and cook for 15 minutes, or until the potatoes are soft. Stir through the parsley and season again with salt and pepper if needed.
3 Stir through the cream (if using), ladle into bowls, and serve with fresh crusty bread.

serves 8

**prep 15 mins
• cook 25 mins**

**freeze for up to
3 months**

Pea and mint soup

This no-cook soup preserves the fresh taste of its ingredients.

INGREDIENTS

250g (9 oz) frozen peas, such as
  petit pois
450ml (15fl oz) hot vegetable stock
handful of mint leaves, roughly chopped
a few thyme stalks, leaves picked
salt and freshly ground black pepper
1–2 tbsp crème fraîche (optional)
pinch of freshly grated nutmeg

METHOD

1 Put the peas in a bowl, pour over boiling water, and leave to stand for about
  5 minutes. Drain.
2 Using a blender, whiz the peas, stock, and herbs until smooth and combined.
  You may have to do this in batches. Add more stock if the soup is too thick. Season
  well with salt and pepper, and whiz again.
3 To serve, stir through the crème fraîche (if using), and top with a pinch of nutmeg. Serve
  hot or cold with crusty bread.

serves 4

prep 10 mins

blender

Mussels in fennel broth

This fragrant broth with coconut and juicy mussels makes an impressive dish.

INGREDIENTS

1 tbsp olive oil
1 onion, finely chopped
1 fennel bulb, trimmed and finely
  chopped
salt and freshly ground black pepper
2 garlic cloves, grated or finely chopped
2 waxy potatoes, peeled and finely diced
300ml (10fl oz) hot vegetable stock or
  light fish stock
400g can coconut milk
1.35kg (3lb) fresh mussels, scrubbed
  and debearded
handful of basil leaves, torn

METHOD

1 Heat the oil in a large pan over a low heat. Add the onion, fennel, and a pinch of salt, then sweat for about 5 minutes until softened. Add the garlic and potatoes, and cook for a few minutes more, being careful not to allow it to brown at all.

2 Pour in the stock, and bring to the boil. Add the coconut milk, reduce the heat slightly, and simmer gently for about 10 minutes, or until the potatoes are cooked. Bring back to the boil, add the mussels, and put a lid on the pan. Cook for about 5 minutes, until all the mussels are open (discard any that do not).

3 To serve, stir through the basil, taste the broth, and season if needed. Serve immediately.

serves 4

prep 10 mins
• cook 20 mins

before cooking, tap the mussels and discard any that do not close

Chestnut and bacon soup

The crunchy texture and nutty flavour of this soup is very satisfying.

INGREDIENTS

2 tbsp olive oil
2 onions, finely chopped
250g (9 oz) bacon or pancetta, chopped
  into bite-sized pieces
4 garlic cloves, grated or finely chopped
1 tbsp finely chopped rosemary leaves
salt and freshly ground black pepper
3 x 200g packets ready-cooked
  chestnuts, chopped
1.2 litres (2 pints) hot chicken stock

METHOD

1 Heat the oil in a large pan, add the onions, and cook over a low heat for 5–8 minutes, or until soft and translucent. Add the bacon or pancetta and cook for 5 minutes, or until crispy. Stir in the garlic and rosemary, then season well with salt and pepper.

2 Stir in the chestnuts, pour in the stock, and bring to the boil. Lower the heat and simmer for 15–20 minutes. Using a slotted spoon, remove a couple of spoonfuls of the bacon and put to one side. Transfer the rest of the soup to a blender or food processor and whiz until puréed.

3 Transfer back to the pan, season again with salt and pepper if needed, then add the reserved bacon pieces. Add a little hot water if the soup is too thick. Serve with a drizzle of extra virgin olive oil and fresh crusty bread.

serves 8

prep 15 mins • cook 30 mins

blender or food processor

freeze for up to 3 months

Bean and rosemary soup

Simple, hearty soups like this one are great to have on stand-by in the freezer.

INGREDIENTS

2 tbsp olive oil, plus a little extra
(according to taste)
2 onions, finely chopped
salt and freshly ground black pepper
1 tbsp finely chopped rosemary leaves
a few sage leaves, finely chopped
4 celery sticks, finely chopped
3 garlic cloves, grated or finely chopped
2 tbsp tomato purée
2 x 400g cans cannellini beans, drained
and rinsed
1.2 litres (2 pints) hot chicken stock
2.5kg (5¼lb) potatoes, cut into
chunky pieces

METHOD

1 Heat the oil in a large pan, add the onions, and cook over a low heat for 6–8 minutes, or until soft and translucent. Season well with salt and pepper, then stir in the rosemary, sage, celery, and garlic, and cook over a very low heat, stirring occasionally, for 10 minutes.

2 Stir through the tomato purée and beans, add a little more olive oil if you wish, and cook gently for 5 minutes. Pour in the stock, bring to the boil, then add the potatoes and simmer gently for 15 minutes, or until cooked. Taste, and season again with salt and pepper if needed. Add a little hot stock if the soup is too thick. Serve with fresh crusty bread.

serves 8

prep 15 mins
• cook 40 mins

freeze for up to
3 months

Cauliflower soup

The potatoes and cauliflower give this soup a silky texture.

INGREDIENTS

2 tbsp olive oil

2 onions, finely chopped

salt and freshly ground black pepper

3 garlic cloves, grated or finely chopped

4 celery sticks, finely chopped

2 bay leaves

675g (1½lb) potatoes, cut into bite-sized
   pieces

1.4 litres (2½ pints) hot vegetable stock

2 cauliflowers, trimmed and cut into
   florets

drizzle of double cream (optional),
   to serve

METHOD

1 Heat the oil in large pan, add the onions, and cook over a low heat for 6–8 minutes, or until soft and translucent. Season well with salt and pepper, then add the garlic, celery, and bay leaves, and cook for 5 minutes, or until the celery begins to soften. Stir in the potatoes and cook for 5 minutes, then pour in the stock, bring to the boil, and cook for 15 minutes, or until the potatoes are nearly soft.

2 Add the cauliflower and cook for 10 minutes, or until it is soft but not watery. Remove the bay leaves and discard, then transfer the soup to a blender or food processor and whiz until smooth. Add a little more hot stock if it seems too thick. Taste, and season with salt and pepper if needed. Drizzle with double cream (if using), and serve with fresh crusty bread.

serves 8

prep 15 mins
• cook 40 mins

blender or
food processor

freeze for up to
3 months

Black bean and coconut soup

Caribbean flavours make this soup a great
way to start a spicy main course.

INGREDIENTS

2 tbsp olive oil

2 red onions, finely chopped

2 bay leaves

salt and freshly ground black pepper

4 garlic cloves, grated or finely chopped

2 tsp ground cumin

2 tsp ground coriander

1 tsp chilli powder

2 x 400g cans black beans, drained and
   rinsed

1.2 litres (2 pints) hot vegetable stock

400ml can coconut milk

flour tortillas, to serve

METHOD

1 Heat the oil in a large pan, add the onions and bay leaves, and cook over a low heat
  for 6–8 minutes, or until the onions are soft and translucent. Season well with salt
  and pepper. Stir through the garlic, cumin, coriander, and chilli powder and cook for
  a few seconds.

2 Stir through the black beans, then pour in the stock and coconut milk. Bring to the
  boil, then reduce to a simmer and cook for 15–20 minutes. Remove the bay leaves
  and discard, then transfer the rest of the soup to a blender or food processor and
  pulse a couple of times so some of the beans are puréed and some remain whole.
  Add a little more hot stock if it is too thick. Season again with salt and pepper. Serve
  with tortilla triangles.

serves 8

prep 15 mins
• cook 30 mins

blender or
food processor

freeze for up to
3 months

Scotch broth

A traditional, stew-like soup, this is both filling and inexpensive to make.

INGREDIENTS

450g (1lb) neck of lamb
salt and freshly ground black pepper
2 tbsp olive oil
1 onion, finely chopped
4 carrots, finely chopped
4 celery sticks, finely chopped
2.3 litres (4 pints) hot light chicken stock
225g (8 oz) pearl barley
handful of curly-leaf parsley, finely
  chopped

METHOD

1 Put the lamb in a large pan, cover with cold water, and season with salt and pepper. Bring to the boil, then lower the heat and simmer for 30 minutes, or until cooked. Remove with a slotted spoon, leave to cool slightly, then shred and put to one side. Reserve the cooking liquid.

2 Heat the oil in a large pan, add the onion, and cook over a low heat for 5 minutes, or until soft and translucent. Add the carrots and celery, and cook over a very low heat for 10 minutes. Strain the reserved liquid, then add to the pan and pour in the stock. Season with salt and pepper, then add the pearl barley and lamb. Bring to the boil, then reduce to a simmer and cook over a very low heat for 1 hour, or until the pearl barley is cooked. Top up with hot water if it begins to dry out too much. Stir through the parsley, then taste and season again with salt and pepper if needed.

serves 8

prep 20 mins
• cook 1 hr
45 mins

freeze, ensuring
the lamb is covered
with liquid, for up
to 3 months

Asian turkey and noodle soup

A light, fragrant, and restorative broth.

INGREDIENTS

900ml (1½ pints) vegetable stock
2 tbsp soy sauce
1 stalk lemongrass, sliced
2.5cm (1in) piece of fresh root ginger,
   peeled and sliced
2 skinless turkey breast fillets, about
   400g (14 oz) each
300g (10 oz) fine rice noodles
1 red chilli, deseeded and sliced
handful of coriander leaves
pinch of salt

METHOD

1 Heat the vegetable stock in a large saucepan over a medium heat. Once hot, add the soy sauce, lemongrass, ginger, and turkey breast fillets. Bring to the boil, reduce the heat slightly, and simmer for 15–20 minutes until the turkey is cooked through. Remove the turkey fillets with a slotted spoon and set aside to cool.
2 To cook the noodles, bring the poaching liquid to the boil, topping up with boiling water if needed. Add the rice noodles and chilli, reduce the heat slightly, and simmer for 1 minute. Shred the turkey and return it to the pan, with the coriander leaves, to heat through. Season with salt to taste, and serve immediately.

serves 4

prep 10 mins,
plus cooling
• cook 30 mins

Chilli beef and bean soup

Spicy Tex-Mex-style flavours are sure to make this soup a favourite.

INGREDIENTS

2 tbsp olive oil
2 onions, finely chopped
salt and freshly ground black pepper
2 red peppers, deseeded and finely
  chopped
2–3 red chillies, deseeded and finely
  chopped
550g (1¼lb) braising steak, cut into
  2.5cm (1in) cubes
1 tbsp plain flour
2.3 litres (4 pints) hot beef stock
2 x 400g cans kidney beans, drained,
  rinsed, and drained again
handful of flat-leaf parsley, finely
  chopped, to serve

METHOD

1 Heat the oil in a large heavy-based pan, add the onions, and cook on a low heat for
  6–8 minutes, or until soft and translucent. Season with salt and pepper, then stir
  through the red peppers and chillies and cook for 5 minutes. Add the meat and cook,
  stirring frequently, for 5–10 minutes, or until beginning to brown all over.
2 Sprinkle in the flour, stir well, and cook for 2 minutes. Add the stock, bring to the boil,
  then cover with a lid and reduce to a simmer. Cook for 1 hour 30 minutes, or until the
  meat is tender. Add the kidney beans and cook for 10 minutes more, then season to
  taste with salt and pepper. Stir through the parsley, and serve.

serves 8

**prep 20 mins
• cook 2 hrs**

**freeze, ensuring the
meat is covered with
liquid, for up to
3 months**

Tomato and chorizo soup

Chickpeas add extra substance to the
Spanish flavours of this soup.

INGREDIENTS

2 tbsp olive oil

250g (9 oz) chorizo, cut into small cubes

2 red onions, finely chopped

4 celery sticks, finely diced

4 carrots, finely diced

3 garlic cloves, grated or finely chopped

salt and freshly ground black pepper

700g jar passata

1.2 litres (2 pints) hot vegetable stock

2 x 400g cans chickpeas, drained and
  rinsed, and drained again

handful of coriander, finely chopped,
  to serve

METHOD

1 Heat half the oil in a large heavy-based pan, add the chorizo, and cook over
  a medium heat, stirring occasionally, for 5 minutes, or until beginning to turn
  crispy. Remove and put to one side.

2 Heat the remaining oil in the pan, add the onions, and cook over a low heat for
  6–8 minutes, or until soft and translucent. Stir in the celery, carrots, and garlic,
  season with salt and pepper, then cook over a low heat, stirring occasionally, for
  8 minutes, or until tender. Add the passata, stock, and chickpeas, and simmer for
  15 minutes. Return the chorizo to the pan, then taste and season with salt and
  pepper if needed. Stir through the coriander and serve.

serves 8

prep 20 mins
• cook 40 mins

freeze for up to
3 months

Potato and leek soup

A simple soup using ingredients available year-round.

INGREDIENTS

450g (1lb) floury potatoes, peeled
1 tbsp olive oil
1 onion, finely chopped
4 leeks, cleaned and sliced
salt and freshly ground black pepper
900ml (1½ pints) hot vegetable stock
small handful of thyme leaves

METHOD

1 Boil the potatoes in a pan of salted water for 15–20 minutes until soft. Drain, then cut into bite-sized pieces.
2 Heat the olive oil in a large pan over a low heat. Add the onion, and sweat gently for about 5 minutes until soft and translucent. Add the leeks, and cook for a further 5 minutes. Season well with salt and pepper. Pour in the hot vegetable stock, and bring to the boil. Reduce the heat slightly, and simmer for about 10 minutes. Add the potatoes, and sprinkle in the thyme leaves. Continue cooking the soup until the potatoes are heated through, then serve hot with some fresh crusty bread.

serves 4

prep 5 mins
• cook 40 mins

Spiced butternut squash soup

You could use any winter squash for this spicy, comforting soup.

INGREDIENTS

2 tbsp olive oil
2 onions, finely chopped
salt and freshly ground black pepper
3 garlic cloves, grated or finely chopped
4 sage leaves, finely chopped
2 red chillies, deseeded and finely chopped
pinch of freshly grated nutmeg

1 large butternut squash or 2 small ones, halved, peeled, deseeded, and chopped into small pieces
2 potatoes, peeled and diced
1.4 litres (2½ pints) hot vegetable stock
chilli oil, to serve
grated Gruyère cheese, to serve

METHOD

1 Heat the oil in a large pan, add the onions, and cook over a low heat for 6–8 minutes, or until soft and translucent. Season with salt and black pepper, then stir through the garlic, sage, chillies, and nutmeg, and cook for a few seconds.

2 Stir in the squash, add the potatoes and stock, and bring to the boil. Reduce to a simmer and cook for 20–30 minutes, or until the squash and potatoes are soft. Transfer to a blender or food processor and whiz until smooth. Taste, and season again with salt and pepper. Serve with a drizzle of chilli oil, and a sprinkling of Gruyère cheese.

serves 8

prep 20 mins
• cook 40 mins

blender or food processor

freeze for up to 3 months

Split pea and bacon soup

This thick soup is a pleasure to eat. The bacon adds flavour, but can be left out for vegetarians.

INGREDIENTS

2 tbsp olive oil

425g (15 oz) bacon or pancetta, chopped
  into bite-sized pieces

2 onions, finely chopped

salt and freshly ground black pepper

4 celery sticks, finely chopped

4 carrots, finely chopped

550g (1¼lb) yellow split peas

1.7 litres (3 pints) hot vegetable stock

METHOD

1 Heat half the oil in a large heavy-based pan, add the bacon or pancetta, and cook over a medium heat, stirring occasionally, for 5 minutes, or until crispy and golden. Remove with a slotted spoon and put to one side. Heat the remaining oil in the pan, add the onions, and cook over a low heat for 6–8 minutes, or until soft and translucent. Season with salt and pepper, then add the celery and carrots and cook on a low heat for 5 minutes.

2 Add the peas and stock and bring to the boil slowly. Cover with a lid, reduce to a simmer, and cook for 2 hours, or until the peas are tender. Check occasionally, and top up with hot water if the soup begins to look too thick. Transfer to a blender or food processor and whiz until smooth and blended. Return to the pan with the bacon or pancetta, then season with salt and pepper to taste. Serve with fresh crusty bread.

serves 8

prep 15 mins
• cook 2 hrs
20 mins

blender or
food processor

freeze for up to
3 months

INDEX

Entries in *italics* indicate
techniques

A

Asian turkey and noodle soup
82
avocados: Chicken noodle soup
63

B

bacon
Chestnut and bacon soup 72
New England clam chowder 52
Split pea and bacon soup 92
White bean soup 34
beans
Bean and rosemary soup 74
Black bean and coconut soup
79
Chilli beef and bean soup 84
Minestrone 50
Tuscan bean soup 44
White bean soup 34
beef
Brown meat stock 15
Chilli beef and bean soup 84
Hungarian goulash soup 47
beetroot: Borscht 23
Black bean and coconut soup
79
Borscht 23
Bouillabaisse 56
bread
French onion soup 48
Porcini mushroom soup 32
Tuscan bean soup 44
Brown meat stock 15
Butternut squash: Spiced
butternut squash soup 90

C

cannellini beans
Bean and rosemary soup 74
Minestrone 50
White bean soup 34
carrots
Brown meat stock 15
Carrot and orange soup 31
Cock-a-leekie soup 55

Curried parsnip soup 20
Lentil soup 64
Minestrone 50
Scotch broth 80
Split pea and bacon soup 92
Thick vegetable soup 39
Tomato and chorizo soup 87
Tuscan bean soup 44
Vegetable stock 8
Winter vegetable soup 58
Cauliflower soup 76
celery
Bean and Rosemary soup 74
Cauliflower soup 76
Lentil soup 64
Minestrone 50
Mushroom soup 28
Scotch broth 80
Split pea and bacon soup 92
Thick vegetable soup 39
Tomato and chorizo soup 87
Tomato soup 26
Vegetable stock 8
cheese
French onion soup 48
Sopa de tortilla 60
Stracciatella with pasta 42
White bean soup 34
Chestnut and bacon soup 72
chicken
Chicken noodle soup 63
chicken stock, making 6
Chicken stock 10
Cock-a-leekie soup 55
chickpeas: Tomato and
chorizo soup 87
chillies
Chicken noodle soup 63
Chilli beef and bean soup 84
Sopa de tortilla 60
Spiced butternut squash soup
90
chorizo: Tomato and
chorizo soup 87
Cock-a-leekie soup 55
coconut milk
Black bean and coconut soup
79
Mussels in fennel broth 71

courgettes: Thick vegetable
soup 39
cucumbers: Gazpacho 16
Curried parsnip soup 20

E

eggs: Stracciatella with pasta 42

F

fennel
Bouillabaisse 56
Fish soup with saffron
and fennel 40
Lobster bisque 36
Mussels in fennel broth 71
fish and seafood
Bouillabaisse 56
Fish soup with saffron
and fennel 40
fish stock, making 7
Fish stock 12
Lobster bisque 36
Mussels in fennel broth 71
New England clam chowder 52
French onion soup 48

G

Gazpacho 16

H

Hungarian goulash soup 47

K

kidney beans: Chilli beef and
bean soup 84

L

lamb
Brown meat stock 15
Scotch broth 80
leeks
Cock-a-leekie soup 55
Potato and leek soup 88
Vegetable stock 8
Vichyssoise 24
Lentil soup 64
Lobster bisque 36

M
Minestrone 50
mushrooms
  Mushroom soup 28
  Porcini mushroom soup 32
mussels
  Bouillabaisse 56
  Fish soup with saffron
    and fennel 40
  Mussels in fennel broth 71

N
New England clam chowder 52
noodles
  Chicken noodle soup 63
  Asian turkey and noodle soup
    82

O
onions: French onion soup 48
oranges: Carrot and orange
  soup 31

P
parsnips: Curried parsnip soup
  20
pasta
  Minestrone 50
  Stracciatella with pasta 42
Pea and mint soup 68
pearl barley: Scotch broth 80
pears: Watercress soup 18
peppers
  Chilli beef and bean soup 84
  Gazpacho 16
  Porcini mushroom soup 32

potatoes
  Bean and rosemary soup 74
  Cauliflower soup 76
  Curried parsnip soup 20
  Fish soup with saffron
    and fennel 40
  Mushroom soup 28
  Mussels in fennel broth 71
  New England clam chowder 52
  Potato and leek soup 88
  Spiced butternut squash soup
    90
  Sweetcorn chowder 66
  Vichyssoise 24
  Winter vegetable soup 58
prawns
  Bouillabaisse 56
  Fish soup with saffron
    and fennel 40

R
rice: Cock-a-leekie soup 55

S
Scotch broth 80
Sopa de tortilla 60
Spiced butternut squash soup
  90
spinach: Tuscan bean soup 44
Split pea and bacon soup 92
stocks
  Brown meat stock 15
  chicken stock, making 6
  Chicken stock 10
  fish stock, making 7
  Fish stock 12
  Vegetable stock 8

Stracciatella with pasta 42
sweet potatoes: Winter
  vegetable soup 58
Sweetcorn chowder 66

T
Thick vegetable soup 39
tomatoes
  Borscht 23
  Bouillabaisse 56
  Chicken noodle soup 63
  Gazpacho 16
  Hungarian goulash soup 47
  Lobster bisque 36
  Minestrone 50
  Porcini mushroom soup 32
  Sopa de tortilla 60
  Thick vegetable soup 39
  Tomato and chorizo soup 87
  Tomato soup 26
  Tuscan bean soup 44
turkey: Asian turkey and noodle
  soup 82
Tuscan bean soup 44

V
Vegetable stock 8
Vichyssoise 24

W
Watercress soup 18
White bean soup 34
Winter vegetable soup 58

London, New York, Melbourne, Munich, and Delhi

Senior Editor Ros Walford

Editorial Assistant Shashwati Tia Sarkar

Designer Elma Aquino

Jacket Designer Mark Penfound

Senior DTP Designer David McDonald

Production Editor Kavita Varma

Indexer Marie Lorimer

DK INDIA

Editorial Consultant Dipali Singh

Designer Neha Ahuja

DTP Designer Tarun Sharma

DTP Coordinator Sunil Sharma

Head of Publishing Aparna Sharma

First published in Great Britain in 2012.
Material in this publication was previously published
in *The Cooking Book, 2008* and *Cook Express, 2009*
by Dorling Kindersley Limited
80 Strand, London WC2R 0RL

Penguin Group (UK)

Copyright © 2008, 2009, 2012 Dorling Kindersley
Text copyright © 2008, 2009, 2012 Dorling Kindersley

10 9 8 7 6 5 4 3 2
002-176927-May/12

A CIP catalogue record for this book is available from the
British Library.

ISBN 978-1-4093-7494-7

Printed and bound by Hung Hing, China.